PLAY BY PLAY

FIGURE SKATING

Figure skating coach Gailene Norwood and the following athletes were photographed for this book:
Viktors Bariss-Ayele,
Elizabeth Burke,
Eva Caruso,
Rachel Cooper,
Vinesha Devandran,
Jessica Hutchens,
Justin Hutchens,
Erin Kilbury,
Tyler Kilbury,
Kristina Litwinczuk,
Carolyn Stephenson,
Breezy Tushaus,
Rohene Ward.

LERNER
SPORTS
AN IMPRINT OF LERNER PUBLISHING GROUP

PLAY BY PLAY

FIGURE SKATING

Joan Freese

Photographs by Andy King

LernerSports ● Minneapolis

To Mark, my first skating coach.

Special thanks to Beth, Natalie, and Shoshana Daniels; Parade Ice Garden staffers Char Martin, Mike Luedtke, and Monica Nybeck; the Parade Figure Skating Club; Becky Headline; The Breck Ice Arena staff; Gailene Norwood; and the talented young athletes who were photographed for this book:

Viktors Bariss-Ayele
Elizabeth Burke
Eva Caruso
Rachel Cooper
Vinesha Devandran
Jessica Hutchens
Justin Hutchens

Erin Kilbury
Tyler Kilbury
Kristina Litwinczuk
Carolyn Stephenson
Breezy Tushaus
Rohene Ward

This book is available in two editions:
Library binding by LernerSports
Soft cover by First Avenue Editions
Imprints of Lerner Publishing Group
241 First Avenue North
Minneapolis, MN 55401 U.S.A.

Website address: www.lernerbooks.com

Library of Congress Cataloging-in-Publication Data

Freese, Joan.
    Play-by-play figure skating / by Joan Freese; photographs by Andy King.
        p.   cm. — (Play-by-play)
    Includes bibliographical references (p.) and index.
    Contents: How this sport got started—Equipment and training—Basics—Advanced technique—Razzle dazzle—Figure skating talk.
    ISBN: 0–8225–3934–7 (lib. bdg. : alk. paper)
    ISBN: 0–8225–0529–0 (pbk. : alk. paper)
    1. Skating—Juvenile literature. [1. Ice skating.
2. Skating.] I. King, Andy, ill. II. Title. III. Series.
GV850.223.F74 2004
796.91—dc21   2002152145

Manufactured in the United States of America
1 2 3 4 5 6 – JR – 09 08 07 06 05 04

Photo Acknowledgments
All attempts have been made to obtain permission from the models in the images of this book. If your image appears without proper credit, please contact Lerner Publishing Group.

Additional photographs are reproduced with the permission of: United States Figure Skating Association, pp. 8, 9 (both), 10, 12 (bottom), 35; © Hulton/Archive by Getty Images, p. 11; © Allsport Hulton Deutsch/Getty Images, p. 12 (top); © Clive Brunskill/Getty Images, pp. 13 (top), 56 (right); SportsChrome East/West, Rob Tringali, p. 13 (bottom left & right), 59; Corbis Royalty Free Images, p. 18 (top right); © Todd Strand/Independent Picture Service, p. 18 (bottom); © Donald Miralle/Getty Images, p. 54; SportsChrome East/West, Bob Tringali, p. 57.
All illustrations by Bill Hauser.

CONTENTS

Chapter 1

HOW THIS SPORT GOT STARTED

Imagine gliding across an ice rink at top speed. With a deep bend of your knee, you push off, leave the ice, and turn one and one-half times in the air before returning to the surface. You land on a metal blade, not much bigger than a dinner knife. And, yes, you're now skating backward!

You've just completed an **Axel**, one of the most difficult jumps in the sport of figure skating. Few other sports combine so completely the strength of athletics with the artistry of dance. It's no wonder that figure skating is popular throughout much of the world.

The great thing about skating is that even if you never try an Axel, the sport presents plenty of challenges. Acquiring the basic skills of figure skating—such as **stroking,** using **edges,** turning, and stopping—requires hours of determined practice on the ice.

GO FIGURE: HOW THE SPORT GOT ITS NAME

Figure skating takes its name from the figures, or patterns, that skaters carve into the ice with their blades. Compulsory figures, which are also called school figures, consist of about forty designs based on the shape of the number 8.

Carlo Fassi, the great figure skating coach who worked with champions like Peggy Fleming and Dorothy Hamill, once said, "Figures are to free skating what bar exercises are to ballet and scales are to piano playing." That is, they are essential routines for mastering more complex aspects of the sport.

Figures were the most important aspect of skating throughout much of the sport's history. They gradually lost importance. In 1990 compulsory figures were dropped from competition entirely. Still, the name remains attached to the sport, pointing to its origins.

Whether pursued recreationally or competitively, figure skating offers something for just about everyone. After learning the basics of moving on the ice, athletes can skate as **singles** or in **pairs**. They can pursue **ice dancing** or **precision skating**, a team event. The skills you learn as a young person can be enjoyed and enhanced throughout the rest of your life.

THE HISTORY OF FIGURE SKATING

The roots of figure skating are very old. People have been ice skating for more than four thousand years. Early skaters, however, did not perform fancy moves in glittery costumes. Rather, the people of northern Europe skated as a practical way to travel across frozen rivers and lakes during hunting trips.

The first skates were made of animal bone. People used them with large sticks, like modern ski poles. Around A.D. 200, iron arrived in Scandinavia. The metal was fashioned into blades, which were tied to a person's feet with leather straps. By the 1400s, people

from the Netherlands attached the blades to their wooden clogs. This crude version resembled modern skates. The Dutch skaters crisscrossed the region's numerous frozen canals as a practical mode of transportation and as a competitive sport.

Skating appeared in other parts of Europe as well. The first recorded skating club was established in Edinburgh, Scotland, in 1784. Early clubs encouraged participation in the sport and organized competitions. But ice skating had also developed into a recreational activity. People

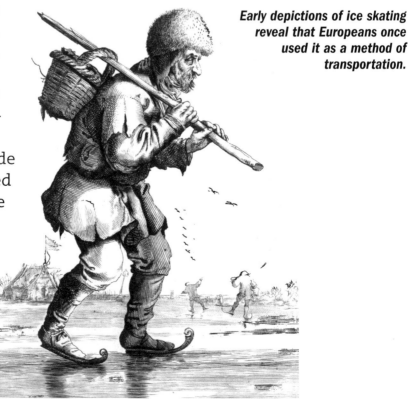

Early depictions of ice skating reveal that Europeans once used it as a method of transportation.

began gathering at the rinks to social-ize and meet new people. By the 1800s, ice skating was a popular pas-time throughout Europe and the United States. To further their skills, skaters concentrated on mastering set patterns—called figures—in the ice. Executing figures with utmost precision and control was a hallmark of the English style of skating.

Ice skating became an acceptable activity for dating.

VITA LYDWINA

Skating was so central to their culture that Dutch artists por-trayed skaters in their works. The earliest known artwork of this kind is a woodcut, dated 1498, by Johannes Brugman. Titled *Vita Lydwina*, the piece shows a teenage girl, Lydwina, who was injured while skating. Upon her death, years later, Lydwina became the patron saint of skaters. Skating is the only sport with its own patron saint.

Jackson Haines changed all that. A ballet dancer from the United States, Haines introduced ballet moves to the sport. His sense of showmanship changed skating into a spectator sport. People became interested in watching accomplished skaters execute feats of great beauty. Haines's brand of skating became known as the International style.

By 1896 the first world championship was held in Russia. It only featured men, but women were not far behind. In 1906 women competed at the world championship. Pairs were added to the roster in 1908.

The first artificial ice rink appeared in Vancouver, Canada, in 1912. This invention made it possible to practice and perform year-round. The extra time advanced the technical elements of the sport. It helped figure skating gain popularity in other ways as well. Indoor ice encouraged the growth of ice shows, or follies. The shows were popular in New York and elsewhere starting around 1915. People rushed to see the skating stars of the time. The accomplished techniques of the athletes wowed audiences.

Figure skating has long been a sport that has embraced women athletes. Taken in 1908, this photo shows women skating at a time when most sports were considered inappropriate for women.

A champion figure skater, Sonja Henie followed up her Olympic success with a career in the movies.

Of all the ice show stars in the history of figure skating, Norwegian champion Sonja Henie was the best known. Henie won Olympic gold medals in 1928, 1932, and 1936. She dominated the world championships for a full decade. Upon retiring from the amateur ranks, Henie pursued the professional skating circuit with vigor. Her name became synonymous with the sport. She brought ice skating to the big screen. Henie starred in eight Hollywood films in the 1930s and 1940s and became a popular movie star. Henie helped the world's elite champions earn high salaries.

Dick Button

Peggy Fleming

As with film, television made megastars of generations of figure skaters. U.S. skater Dick Button dazzled the world in the 1940s and 1950s. California darling Peggy Fleming brought cool sophistication to the sport in the 1960s.

Perky Dorothy Hamill dominated the media in the 1970s. American skaters Scott Hamilton and Brian Boitano dominated the men's competitions throughout the 1980s, while Kristi Yamaguchi and Tara Lipinski captured Olympic gold—and the media spotlight—during the 1990s.

Audiences worldwide tune in to see the most accomplished athletes in the history of skating. Figure skating features glamour, artistry, and athletic prowess. Champions with these skills are rewarded with professional contracts.

The United States Figure Skating Association (USFSA) has over 155,000 members and has grown by nearly 50,000 members in the past decade! More than 1,300 skating competitions are held in the United States alone each year. Figure skating's importance in the sporting world speaks to the unmatched combination of athletic strength and artistic beauty.

Michelle Kwan

Dorothy Hamill

Timothy Goebel

Chapter 2

EQUIPMENT AND TRAINING

Learning to skate calls for some basic equipment and, most likely, a few lessons. Figure skates and ice are the only two requirements for skating. Most organized programs are held at indoor rinks. Artificial ice provides a more consistent surface that is easier to maintain. Local telephone directories help in locating nearby rinks.

Figure skates can be expensive. Renting skates allows beginners to try the sport without investing too much money. Many rinks offer affordable skate rental. Parents may also consider skate swaps and used sporting goods shops. Young feet grow quickly. This year's boots may be too small by next year's skating season. When buying skates, there are a number of things to consider.

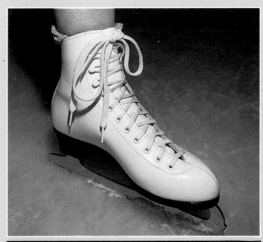

LACING YOUR SKATES

When lacing skates, the first three or four eyelets of the skate, those nearest the toe, should be tied comfortably but not too tightly. Skaters should be able to wiggle their toes in fully laced skates. From the arch of the foot to just about the ankle, the laces should be pulled tightly to offer firm ankle support. At the top of the skate, where the eyelets are replaced by hooks, laces should be pulled firmly but with some give.

15

SKATES

Figure skates are composed of two parts: boots and blades. Beginners do not require the most expensive equipment, but their skates should fit properly. Avoid oversized boots, which can make a skater feel unstable and increase the chance of injury. Skates should fit snugly but comfortably.

How do skaters know if they have the correct fit? When standing in laced skates, athletes should be able to wiggle their toes but not lift their heels. In addition, skaters shouldn't have any movement around the insteps (arches) of their feet. Firm boots provide support for landing jumps with force. If boots fit correctly and are laced properly, skaters should never feel they have weak ankles. Experiencing weak ankles is a warning sign that the skates aren't properly fitted.

The best boots are made of leather. A recreational skater who doesn't skate every day and whose feet have stopped growing can expect to keep a pair of boots for many years.

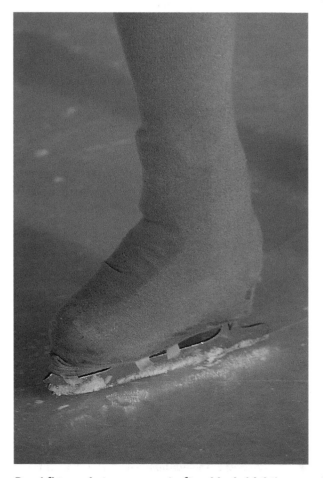

Boys' figure skates are most often black (right). Girls' figure skates are white or tan. Competitive skaters may wear boot covers to match their costumes without the expense of new boots.

space. At the front, near the toe, the blade is jagged. This area is the toe pick. While beginners do not often use their toe picks, more advanced skaters do for certain jumps and spins.

Blades need to be sharpened from time to time. Instructors can help beginners recognize when their skates need sharpening. Eventually, regular skaters can gauge their own blades by running a fingernail along the edges. If the nail glides along the blade smoothly, without a nick, the blades need to be sharpened. Skates are sharpened by craftspeople who are specially trained. Skate shops and the local rink are good places to look for sharpening services.

When not on the ice, skaters cover their blades with rubber skate guards (left). They protect blades from the wear and tear of hard surfaces like concrete and wood. When finished for the day, skaters dry their blades with a towel to prevent rust and put terry cloth covers, called "soakers" or "cozies," on the blades.

Some skaters will need blades specially made for their area of the sport. Ice dancers and pair skaters use blades that accommodate their unique skating moves. For example, dance blades are shorter in the back than regular figure skate blades. This alteration helps to prevent partners skating close together from stepping on each other's blades.

BLADES

The bottom of a figure skate blade is not flat. It has two edges—an inside edge and an outside edge. In between the edges is a hollow, or concave,

NAME THAT BLADE!

One of the most basic differences between figure skates and those used for hockey or speed skating is the blades. Figure skates (top left) have slightly curved blades, with two edges and a toe pick. The blades of hockey skates (bottom left) do not have toe picks. But they do have heel guards, which prevent injury in rough and tumble games. Speed skates (top right) have long, thin blades that are also without toe picks. Longer blades make for faster travel across the ice. Speed skating boots rest lower on the ankle than figure skating and hockey boots.

WHAT DO FIGURE SKATERS WEAR?

Figure skaters' clothes depend on whether they skate indoors or outdoors. When skating indoors, athletes want to stay warm without overdressing. It's a good idea to layer garments so skaters can adjust their clothes to fit rink conditions and their workout.

For practicing, leggings and sweatpants are the best options. Worn over a lightweight shirt, a jacket or sweater can be removed after the skater has warmed up.

Skaters should avoid wearing loose clothing. Long pants or loose scarves could become entangled and cause a fall. Most skaters wear gloves to avoid "ice burns" when falling down. And they avoid thick, wool socks. Thin socks don't interfere with a skate's tightness.

For competitive events, skaters must adhere to dress codes. Girls are required to wear tights, for example. As skaters progress to competitions, their coaches can offer tips for appropriate dress.

The perfect practice outfit includes a removable outer layer, such as a jacket.

Costumes for competitive events can be custom-made, rented, or handed down.

LESSONS

Because skating is a highly technical sport, lessons are required to build sound fundamental skills and to avoid developing bad habits. In the United States, two major skating organizations promote the sport by offering lessons. Both the USFSA and the Ice Skating Institute (ISI) have excellent programs with standards that skaters must master before advancing to the next level of study. To verify that they are ready for such a move, skaters must pass tests. During a test session, students perform specific skills before a skating expert, who confirms that they have mastered the necessary skills.

How do the two programs differ? In general, USFSA is known as the program for serious skaters who wish to compete on the national level and have such aspirations as reaching the Olympics. The ISI program targets recreational skaters. Both programs are very well respected. In fact, it's not unusual for young skaters to participate in both programs.

Group lessons are sufficient for beginners. As a skater becomes more serious, individual lessons may be required. Professional coaches, or pros, can tailor lessons to the individual needs of a skater. This kind of personalized attention can make for faster progress in the sport.

SKATING CLUBS

Committed skaters may require individual ice time to achieve their goals. Skating clubs are good places to find coaches and to gain access to ice. Skating clubs rent rinks. They then resell the ice time to club members, who use the time to work on their individual skills. Clubs put on events, such as ice shows and exhibitions, which give athletes experience skating in front of crowds. Clubs also organize competitions during which members can skate against their peers.

PRACTICE

Mastering the sport of figure skating requires a lot of time on the ice. Skating during recreational sessions can strengthen the skills learned in class. These informal sessions allow skaters to practice skills from class, learn moves from friends, and see more advanced skaters in action. Recreational skating sessions are relaxing times to have fun on the ice—and that's what figure skating is all about.

BASICS

Beginning skaters should work hard to learn the basics. These fundamentals are building blocks for the fancy moves that make the sport exciting.

To make skating instructions clear, body parts are referred to very specifically in figure skating. When skating, the foot on the ice is called the **skating foot**. The foot off the ice is called the **free foot**. For example, in the photo on the right, Vinesha's right foot is her skating foot. In addition, her right leg is her skating leg and her right arm is her skating arm. Because Vinesha's left foot is off the ice, it's her free foot. Her left leg is her free leg and her left arm is her free arm.

The first time on the ice, skaters should begin by simply walking in their skates with arms extended at their sides for balance. Walking gives beginners a feel for the ice and their blades. When entering a rink, remember to skate with the flow of traffic and to be on the lookout for other skaters. Experienced skaters will be able to move around beginners. But keeping an eye out for others on the ice is part of the sport, and skaters should practice the skill from the start.

Vinesha's coach reminds her that she should be pointing the toe of her free foot out to the side. To do so, Vinesha will rotate her leg from the hip socket so her whole leg turns out.

23

It's natural to feel more comfortable along the boards, or the walls, of the rink. However, try not to rely on the wall too much. Some little children learn to move on the ice with a chair or a special frame as their support. While this is fine for absolute beginners, it's always best to learn to balance on your own as soon as possible.

SCULLING

Once a skater has mastered walking on the ice, it's time to try **sculling**. Sculling is the in-and-out movement of one's blades. This simple motion propels a skater across the ice.

To begin sculling forward (*figure 1*), the skater's feet are side by side with the toes pointed out. The arms are extended at the sides to help with balance. The skater then bends the knees and pushes the toes apart. When the skater's feet are a couple of feet from each other (*figure 2*), the skater turns the toes inward (*figure 3*) and returns to the original position.

To scull backward, reverse the process. Beginning with the toes together and heels pointed out, bend your knees and push your heels outward. Next, curve your heels together and then apart again.

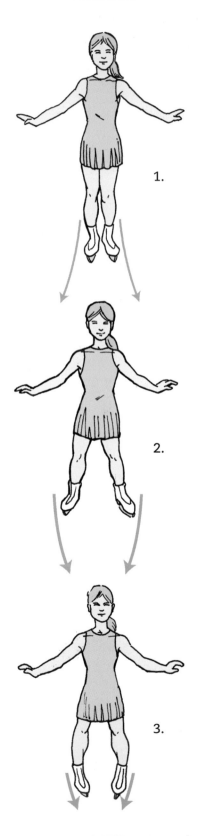

1.

2.

3.

FORWARD STROKE

Stroking is the basic movement of figure skating. Breezy begins her forward stroke by pushing off with the full inside edge of her free foot. This edge is placed on the ice at a 45-degree angle to her skating foot. It's important to point the toe of the free foot. It's natural for beginners to want to push off with their toe picks. But try not to use the toe picks to either start or stop. This bad habit is not compatible with correct skating form.

As Breezy pushes off using her free foot, she bends her skating knee. She then glides on her skating foot and brings her free foot in front of her body. Breezy then transfers her weight to this foot, bending her knee as she does. The bending and straightening of the skating knee is where the power of the stroke is found.

Notice Breezy's arms. They're extended to her sides to help with balance. Don't worry. Like riding a bike, skating will begin to feel natural as more time is spent on the ice. Just remember to bend those knees and keep your back upright.

Forward Stroke

Forward left outside edge

Backward left inside edge

EDGES

Almost everything about skating technique depends on being on the correct edge at the correct time. But beginning skaters may not be able to tell if they are on an edge. The ice says it all. If a blade is flat on the ice, it will leave two parallel tracings, or marks. When on an edge, the blade leaves just a single tracing in the ice.

Although compulsory figures are no longer part of the sport, learning to use edges never goes out of style. There are eight basic edges to master: left forward outside, right forward outside, left forward inside, right forward inside, left backward outside, right backward outside, left backward inside, and right backward inside. Got that? These names may sound complicated, but they simply describe the foot being used, the direction being skated, and the edge of the blade being employed.

Learning to use your edges may seem tedious to a young skater. But using them well is essential for mastering fun moves such as jumps and spins.

FORWARD CROSSOVERS

A **crossover** is a stroke made in order to skate in a circle. Here, Vinesha skates counterclockwise. She performs a crossover by placing her outside foot in front of her skating foot. As she turns, her weight transfers from her left forward outside edge (the foot being crossed) to her right forward inside edge (the foot crossing over).

Forward Crossover

Backward Crossover

BACKWARD CROSSOVERS

Backward crossovers may take a little longer to master than forward, but you'll be skating in circles in no time! Erin performs a backward crossover in the counterclockwise direction. While gliding backward on her right foot, she crosses her left foot in front of her right, taking an inside edge.

Once the weight transfers to the left foot, the right foot executes a push-off before returning to the ice, a bit behind her left foot. Additional crossovers are performed in the same fashion to complete the circle. When performing backward crossovers, as with front crossovers, the foot being crossed over is on the outside edge while the foot crossing over is on the inside edge.

STOPPING

After skaters are able to move freely on the ice, they discover a little secret of the sport. Learning to stop is every bit as important as learning to go!

The snowplow stop is a favorite for beginners because it's easy to per-form. The basic idea should be familiar to people who ski. Gliding on her left foot, Rachel places her right foot in front at an angle. Slowly transferring her weight to her right foot brings her to a stop as the blade pushes into the ice. Snowplow stops can be performed on either foot.

*Snowplow
Stop*

T-Stop

Hockey Stop

When performing a t-stop, the skater's blades form a "T." Gliding forward on her left foot, Rachel places her right foot behind her left at a 90-degree angle. As she does, her weight changes from her left foot to the outside edge of her right foot. Rachel is careful not to step on the back of her left foot blade when performing this stop. Doing so guarantees a fall!

A hockey stop can be done at high speeds and is thus popular among hockey players. But figure skaters like it, too! Rachel executes a hockey stop by bending both knees and turning her heels to the right. While her feet are parallel to one another, her upper body will go from being aligned with her lower body to ending at a 90-degree angle.

TURNS

In skating, turns are used to change direction from skating forward to backward or from skating backward to forward. Once you learn to turn the three-turn (below) and the mohawk, you're sure to notice how often advanced skaters use these common turns to get into position for jumps and spins.

The easiest one-foot turn is the three-turn, so called because it leaves a shape like the number three traced in the ice. A total of eight different three-turns are possible. Three-turns can be executed to the right and the left while skating forward or backward. And three-turns can be done on the outside or inside edges. Here, the diagram shows a forward left outside three-turn. Notice the carriage of the upper body. Correctly positioning arms and shoulders will help execute the turn with ease.

THREE-TURN

1.   2.   3.   4.

A mohawk is a two-foot turn done on a curve, from an inside edge to an inside edge or from an outside edge to an outside edge. The skater in the illustration below is doing an inside mohawk. The skater begins on the right forward inside edge (*figure 1*). The skater's body rotates along the curve. Next the skater lifts the free foot and positions it along the same curve (*figure 2*). The skater then places the left foot on the ice, with the heel turned toward the toe of the right foot (*figure 3*). The skater lifts the right foot off the ice and continues by skating backward on the left foot (*figure 4*).

MOHAWK

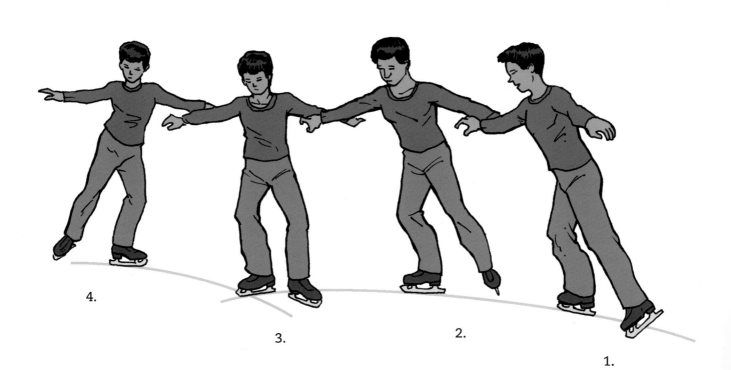

4.

3.

2.

1.

OUCH!

As funny as it may seem, learning to fall correctly is an important part of learning to skate. Tumbling on the ice is inevitable for both beginners and advanced skaters. Relax, it's very rare for a skater to be seriously injured because of a fall. In fact, falling on the ice has advantages over falling on the ground. On the ice, the impact of the fall is dispersed over a greater distance, because the skater slides across the ice.

If possible, it's best to land on one's backside. To stand up, Breezy positions herself on her hands and knees. She steadies one foot on the ice, then the other, and eases into a standing position. If the fall is really hard, Breezy takes a few minutes to regain her composure, leaving the ice if necessary. In general, she doesn't mind a slip or two because, as her teacher often reminds her, "You can't learn to skate if you don't fall down."

Chapter 4

ADVANCED TECHNIQUE

So you've mastered the three-turn and are wondering what comes next? Not to worry, skating offers new challenges around each corner—or curve! Spins, jumps, and **footwork** are the basic elements of freestyle skating. Freestyle, which is also called free skating, refers to the kind of figure skating that people see on television. In other words, freestyle skating involves athletes performing routines on the ice, usually to music. These programs show what is best about the sport by combining impressive technical elements with engaging artistic presentation.

WHAT'S IN A NAME?

Some figure skating moves were named for the athletes who invented them. Axel jumps are named after Axel Paulsen (above), a Norwegian skater who competed on the world level in the 1880s. The Salchow took its name from Ulrich Salchow, a Swedish skater who won ten world championships during his career! Dorothy Hamill added a variation to the camel spin that became known as the Hamill camel, while the Biellmann spin got its name from Denise Biellmann, a Swiss skater who invented the exciting move.

SPINS

A skater performs a spin by turning in the same place on the ice—much like a top. Skaters typically have a direction they like to turn. For most right-handed skaters, it's counterclockwise, or spinning to the left. Spins can be divided into three basic groups: upright spins, which are done standing up; camel spins, which are done in an arabesque (bent forward) position; and sit spins, which are done in the sitting position. A combination spin is one that combines several of these spins into a fluid movement on the ice. In a well-executed combination spin, the skater is able to maintain the same speed throughout the entire spin.

The two-foot spin, an upright spin, is the first spin skaters learn. Before the spin, both Erin's feet are on the ice. Her blades are flat, about one foot apart. She begins by "winding up" her torso clockwise. To gain momentum, she twists her upper body the other direction. Her arms are held out as she turns her right foot slightly inward. As she spins, she is on the forward inside edge of her right foot and the backward inside edge of her left foot. In other words, her right foot is going forward and her back foot is going backward. As Erin gains momentum (below), she brings her arms in, as if hugging herself, and releases her upper body so it's directly above her feet.

Two-foot Spin

Scratch Spin

The scratch spin is sometimes called the blur spin. Skaters can perform the move with impressive speed. A scratch spin can be executed turning forward or backward. Here, Eva is performing a forward scratch spin. To gain momentum, her free leg is positioned quite wide. However, as she gains speed, she crosses her free foot in front of her skating foot. The position is used during a back scratch spin as well. During the forward spin, Eva is on a left forward outside edge. During backward spins, she would be on a right backward outside edge. Correct body alignment for both directions includes a straight back and erect head.

A sit spin is executed in the sitting position. Vinesha begins the spin as she would an upright spin. But as she gains speed, she "sits" by bending her skating knee and leaning forward at the waist. While spinning, Vinesha's skating leg is bent and her free leg is extended. Notice how straight she holds her back.

Camel Spin

Sit Spin

A camel spin is done in the arabesque position. Viktors enters the camel as if he's starting an upright spin, but then he quickly assumes the arabesque position. While doing a camel spin, Viktors stretches his free leg straight and centers his weight over his skating foot. He moves his arms during the camel spin primarily to maintain his balance, but it also adds an artistic touch.

The layback spin, which is done with a gracefully arched back, is more common for women. Men rarely perform it. It requires an especially supple back—a quality that is physiologically less likely for men. In this move, it is also very important to push your hips forward in order to execute the spin.

Layback Spin

JUMPS

To many spectators, jumps rank as the most exciting moves in figure skating. But it's often hard for non-skaters to tell one jump from the next. Jumps are distinguished by subtle differences in takeoff and landing. These moves happen so fast that it can be difficult for onlookers to see them—especially when watching world-class figure skaters.

Jumps fall into two categories: edge jumps or toe jumps. Edge jumps use the blade edges for take-off. Loops, Salchows, and Axels are all edge jumps. Toe jumps use the toe pick for takeoff. Lutzes, toe loops, and flips are all toe jumps.

Each jump can be divided into three parts—**approach, airtime,** and landing. The approach includes the moves in which a skater prepares for the jump. Airtime is the time when the actual jump occurs. The landing is when a skater returns to the ice. A clean jump is landed on one foot. Skaters who jump counterclockwise land on their right feet. Clockwise jumpers land on their left feet.

Each jump is learned in the following order: single, double, triple. At the very top level, some skaters attempt quads. Jumps can also be performed in combination (two jumps in a row with no steps between).

This section gives basic descriptions of the single jumps. All jumps can be made into doubles or triples.

Note that while it's interesting to read about jumps, none of them can be learned from a book. Jumps are simply too complex—and danger-ous—to learn without the informed guidance of a skating teacher or coach. But it never hurts to read up on something before trying it.

The waltz jump is a beginner jump. It involves a half rotation in the air. Vinesha performs a waltz jump. She takes off from her left forward out-side edge, turns a half revolution in the air, extends both her legs to the side, and lands on her right backward outside edge. Note that the takeoff foot is different than the landing foot.

Mid-waltz Jump

TOE LOOP JUMP

1.
2.
3.
4.
5.
6.
7.

8.

After the waltz jump, the toe loop is considered the easiest jump. The toe loop is a toe jump. The skater uses the left toe pick (*figures 5 and 6*) and turns to the left. The turn in the air is similar to the waltz jump (*figure 8*). The skater lands on the right foot. Skaters often do three-turns to get into position for toe loops.

9.
10.

FLIP JUMP

The flip is also a toe jump. The skater takes off from the backward inside edge of the left foot. The skater uses the toe pick of the right foot to assist in the jump (*figure 2*). The skater turns to the left and lands the flip on the backward outside edge of the right foot (*figure 5*). Skaters often do three-turns to get into position for flips.

1.

2.

LOOP JUMP

1.

2.

3.

3.

4.

5.

4.

5.

Not to be confused with the toe loop, a loop jump has an edge takeoff instead of a toe takeoff. The skater in the illustration performs a loop jump, taking off from the right backward outside edge. During the turn, the left leg crosses in front of the body (*figure 3*). Before landing, the right leg moves behind the left leg and the arms extend, to help with balance (*figure 4*). The skater lands on the right backward outside edge. Note that in the loop jump, the takeoff and landing foot are the same.

This toe jump, called a lutz, has a takeoff from the backward outside edge of one foot, usually the left, with a toe assist from the other (*figure 2*). A lutz is landed on the right backward outside edge of the assist foot (*figure 6*). The lutz's height is gained from the "toe tap." Nonskaters can often identify this jump because athletes typically perform a backward glide into the corner of the rink before executing a lutz.

LUTZ JUMP

SALCHOW JUMP

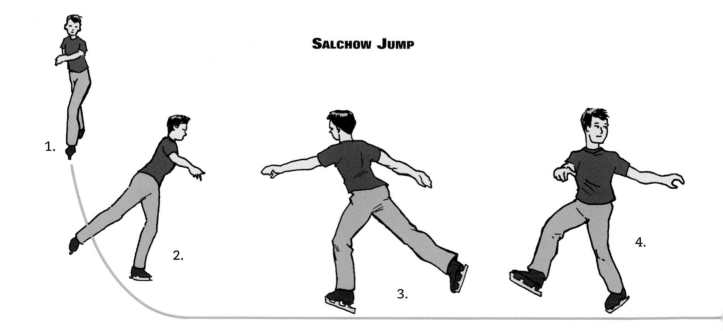

3. 4. 5. 6.

The Salchow is similar to a waltz jump. The skater takes off from the left backward inside edge (*figures 3 and 4*). With a swing of the free leg, the skater turns and lands on the right backward outside edge. When performing a single Salchow, skaters actually turn less than a full 360 degrees. Skaters commonly do mohawks or three-turns to get into position for Salchows.

5. 6. 7.

The Axel is the most difficult single jump. A skater takes off in forward position and completes one and one-half **revolutions** in the air before landing! It is the only jump with a forward takeoff. An Axel takes off from the forward outside edge of the left foot (*figures 2 and 3*) and lands on the backward outside edge of the right foot (*figure 7*).

AXEL JUMP

1.

2.

3.

4.

5.

6.

7.

FOOTWORK

In figure skating, the word *footwork* refers to a series of steps that are put together to show a skater's ability to perform intricate moves on the ice. These steps are done across the ice in straight lines, circular patterns, or three-circle patterns, called serpentines. The footwork portions of programs may not be as exciting as jumps and spins, but they are important opportunities for displaying the strength of one's choreography and artistic expression.

Chapter 5

RAZZLE DAZZLE

After hours and hours of training, many skaters move on to skate in front of an audience. Skating performances include competitions and ice shows, which are typically organized by skating clubs or rinks. Competitions are probably familiar to most skating enthusiasts, because these events are sometimes shown on television. Annual ice shows, which are similar to dance recitals, are opportunities for skating students to show off their hard-earned skills to parents and friends.

Before participating in such events, skaters must decide what kind of skating they want to do. Once a figure skater has mastered the basics, there are many opportunities for specializing within the sport. These different kinds of skating are called disciplines. The five figure skating disciplines are Women's Singles, Men's Singles, Pairs, Ice Dancing, and Precision Skating.

In terms of competitions, each discipline has its own structure and requirements. Even the most avid skating fan sometimes finds the various rules and judging factors confusing. The requirements discussed in this book are for USFSA competitions. These requirements match those typically seen on television in nonprofessional competitive events.

SINGLES

Men and women compete in separate classes by skating a **short** and a **long program**. The short program lasts about two and one-half minutes. During this time, the skater must perform eight required elements—three jumps, three spins, and two steps. The specific required elements change each year. Skaters are judged on required elements and presentation.

The long program, which is also known as the free skate, lasts four and one-half minutes. In this event, skaters perform choreography that expresses their artistry and showcases their technical strengths. While no requirements are given for the free skate, basic guidelines are suggested. Experienced skaters know the elements they will need to include in their free skate to be competitive.

PAIRS

Pairs skating, which features male-female partners, is known for dramatic lifts, throws, spirals, and compelling **unison skating**. Lifts are moves in which the male skater lifts his partner overhead with his arms fully extended. A throw is something like a jump, but the woman is propelled into the air by her partner. With this extra boost, women reach greater heights in throws than they do on their own in jumps.

These pairs skaters, Breezy and Rohene, are performing a spiral and a move called shoot-the-duck.

The most popular spiral in pairs skating is the well-known death spiral, so named because it's quite dangerous to execute. In unison skating, the female and male partners execute the same moves simultaneously. Unison skating has some variations, such as mirror skating, in which the two skaters perform the same moves but in opposite directions, thus mirroring each other. As with singles, pairs skate a short program, based on specific requirements, and a longer free skate.

These skaters are pairs skating. It takes years of practice before pairs can perform lifts and throws. The lifts performed in pairs skating require a great deal of strength on the part of the male skater. It's common for male skaters to use weight training to prepare for this role.

ICE DANCING

Ice dancing is very much what it sounds like—dancing on the ice. Like pairs, it involves a male-female partnership. But ice dancers use music as more than accompaniment to their routines. Moving to dance music is the very essence of ice dancing.

Most lifts and jumps aren't allowed in ice dancing. Yet, ice dancing has its own unique strengths. Ice dancers are known for their ability to execute complicated footwork very near their partners. In addition, ice dancers master (and memorize!) complicated dance patterns that would intimidate even the most accomplished singles skater. With its concentration on musicality and the precise execution of complicated footwork in a fluid fashion, ice dancing is considered by many people to be the absolute height of artistry in figure skating.

During competitions, ice dancers skate four dances. These include two compulsory dances, an original dance, and a free dance. A compulsory dance is one that has prescribed patterns and steps. Each season, four compulsory dances are selected from a total of thirty-one compulsory dances. Each dance pair can execute all of these dances. During each competition, two compulsory dances are drawn from these four. These two are the dances that will be per-

formed by all ice dance couples for the compulsory phase of that competition. Each compulsory dance accounts for 10 percent of a couple's total score.

The original dance happens during the second phase of an ice dance competition. An original dance is a two-minute dance set to a specific rhythm, such as samba or tango, within a set tempo range. Within these guidelines, which are set prior to each competitive season, skaters create their own unique dance. The original dance accounts for 30 percent of an ice dance team's final score.

And, finally, a four-minute free dance, which allows dance couples to demonstrate their creativity and personality, completes the ice dance competition. Couples skate their own routines, which must follow the basic guidelines of ice dancing—that is, they must skate to dance music, with only small jumps, lifts, and spins. The free dance accounts for 50 percent of an ice dance team's final score.

Natalia Gudina and Alexei Beletsky of Israel compete in the dance free skate during the 2002 Salt Lake City Winter Olympics.

PRECISION SKATING

In precision skating, twelve to twenty-four skaters perform choreographed routines on the ice together. This team sport has been compared to synchronized swimming. Both sports involve a highly intricate and disciplined presentation of technique. Included in this technique are five standard formations: circles, blocks, intersections, lines, and wheels. Skaters form circles by linking their arms. Skaters align themselves in rows to form a block. For an intersection, the skating team divides in two, with the first half moving through the second half. Skaters perform lines in one or two straight rows, like a kick line in dance. Wheels are performed in lines that resemble the spokes of a wheel.

Scoring for precision skating is the same as for singles and pairs. Precision skating is not an Olympic sport, though it is being considered for the future.

Competitions happen at all levels. Events for young amateur skaters can be good experience for future skating.

COMPETING

USFSA competitions are open to all members of the organization. To join, a skater must pay basic membership dues. To compete at one of eight levels, skaters must pass tests, which are taken at their USFSA club. Skaters must pass a two-part test to compete at a specific level. Of course, not all USFSA skaters wish to compete. In this case, a skater would test to be allowed into the next level of instruction.

In pairs skating, Canadian skaters Jamie Salé and David Pelletier won a gold medal at the 2002 Winter Olympic Games.

Some moves, such as this back flip done by Surya Bonaly, are not allowed in skating competitions. Skaters sometimes perform them in professional or more informal exhibition events, however.

JUDGES AND SCORING

Compared to sports that have clear-cut winners based on scoring the most points, figure skating is slightly more subjective. After all, the idea is to reward the best skater. Someone must determine who the best skater is. That's the job of figure skating judges. Judges are accustomed to watching the sport and know its many technical facets. They are interested in supporting figure skating by lending their expertise to benefit athletes. It's the judges' job to rank the skaters in terms of how they perform relative to the other skaters in the competition.

So how exactly is figure skating scored? The percentages account for the breakdown of final scores. For example, in singles skating, the short program accounts for 33.3 percent of a skater's final score, while the free skate accounts for 66.7 percent of the final score. Within this breakdown, skaters are judged on two specific things: technical merit and artistic presentation. Scores range from 1 to 6, with 1 being very poor and 6 being perfect. Technical merit scores are given for how well skaters display their skating skills. Artistic presentation scores suggest how beautifully the skater performed.

Obviously, different judges will have different opinions. In fact, during international competitions, the preferences of judges from different cultural backgrounds can be quite pronounced. But for young skaters coming up in the sport, the important thing to remember is that different competitions have different scoring systems. Check with your coach to learn more. Now get on the ice and have some fun!

Coaches are there for skaters during their competitions. They can offer good advice and help skaters calm their nerves.

Olympic gold medalist Alexei Yagudin skates before a panel of judges, who watch each skater's moves very closely.

FIGURE SKATING TALK

airtime: the time a skater spends in the air during a jump

approach: how the skater enters a jump including the footwork and the body's position

Axel: "the king of jumps," in which the skater takes off forward and rotates one and a half turns in the air in order to land on one foot in the backward direction

crossover: crossing one foot over the other in order to turn corners

edge: the outside or inside of a skating blade

footwork: a series of intricate steps that reveal a skater's precision

free foot: the foot that is not on the ice and has no weight on it

ice dancing: a form in figure skating that resembles ballroom dancing. Skating couples move in time to the music while keeping contact with one another.

long program: also known as a free skate, this routine features a skater's artistic or creative moves, which they choose themselves.

pairs: an event in which a male and female skater skate together. The event features overhead lifts, throw-jumps, and other maneuvers.

precision skating: a team sport in which skaters perform choreographed moves at the same time

revolution: a full-circle in a spin

sculling: pushing the feet away and then together to generate movement on the ice

short program: a routine set to music. Also known as the technical program, it is judged on jumps, spins, and footwork.

single jump: any jump in which the skater rotates only once in the air

singles: an event in which women and men skate alone. A singles event has a long and a short program.

skating foot: the foot on the ice that performs the move

stroking: the basic skating movement in which the skater presses the blade of the free foot into the ice in order to push off

unison skating: a form of figure skating in which the female and male partners perform the same moves simultaneously

FURTHER READING

Cranston, Patty. *Magic on Ice*. Tonawanda, NY: Kids Can Press, 1998.

Cranston, Patty. *The Best on Ice: The World's Top Figure Skaters*. Tonawanda, NY: Kids Can Press, 1997.

Fleming, Peggy. *The Official Book of Figure Skating: History, Competition, Technique*. New York: Simon & Schuster, 1998.

Foeste, Aaron. *Ice Skating Basics*. New York: Sterling Publishing, 2000.

Milton, Steve and Gérard Châtaigneau. *Figure Skating Now: Olympic and World Champions*. Westport, CT: Firefly Books, 2001.

Wilkes, Debbi. *The Figure Skating Book*. Westport, CT: Firefly Books, 1999.

Yamaguchi, Kristi. *Figure Skating For Dummies*. Indianapolis, IN: IDG Books Worldwide, 1997.

WEBSITES

International Figure Skating
<http://www.ifsmagazine.com>

International Skating Union
<http://www.isu.org>

Skate Canada
<http://www.skatecanada.ca>

SkateWeb
<http://www.frogsonice.com/skateweb/>

World Figure Skating Museum
<http://www.worldskatingmuseum.org/>

FOR MORE INFORMATION

United States Figure Skating Assoc.
20 First Street
Colorado Springs, CO 80906
www.usfsa.org

Ice Skating Institute
17120 North Dallas Parkway
Dallas, TX 75248-1187
www.skateisi.com

INDEX

ABOUT THE AUTHOR

Joan Freese is a children's writer who works in the educational software market. A former arts writer, Ms. Freese has had her dance writings published in numerous publications, including the *Minneapolis Star Tribune* and *The Village Voice*. She lives in Minneapolis, Minnesota, with her husband and children.